Pocket Guide to the Roman Missal

Jude Valor

Pocket Guide to the Roman Missal: *A Beginner's Guide to the Order of the Catholic Mass and the Prayers, Gestures, and Meaning Behind It*

by
Jude Valor

First Edition: March, 2026
ISBN: 978-93-5779-739-9
Published by: Mittal Enterprises

Contents

Liturgy of the Eucharist

Concluding Rites

PART III — Understanding the Prayers, Gestures, and Meaning

PART IV — Practical Helps for a More Prayerful Mass

PART V — Short Prayers and Devotions

Introduction

Why the Mass Matters

Imagine holding the key to a vast, ancient, and breathtaking treasure chest. You know the treasure is there, but you can't quite figure out how to unlock it, or what to do once the lid is lifted.

For countless Catholics, this feeling describes their experience of the Holy Mass. They know the Mass is the most important thing they do all week, but the ritual, the prayers, the constant standing, sitting, and kneeling, and the ancient language can sometimes leave them feeling like spectators rather than participants.

This pocket guide is the key. It is designed to take the mystery out of the ritual and reveal the incredible depth of reality that is unfolding on the altar every single time you attend Mass.

Why the Mass Is the Heart of Catholic Life

Why do over a billion Catholics worldwide consider

the Mass, formally known as the Eucharistic Celebration, the "source and summit" of their faith? The answer is simple and radical: **The Mass is where heaven and earth meet.**

It is not merely a communal prayer service, a nice tradition, or a gathering to hear Bible stories. The Mass is the singular moment when the eternal sacrifice of Jesus Christ on the cross at Calvary is made present, here and now, for us.

In the Mass, we don't just remember what Jesus did; we enter into it. Every blessing, every Scripture reading, every shared moment of peace, and especially every word of the Eucharistic Prayer, draws us closer to that defining moment of love on the cross and the triumphant joy of the Resurrection. Everything the Catholic Church is, and everything she does, flows from this act of worship and returns to it.

Jesus Truly Present in the Eucharist

At the core of the Catholic faith is the astounding claim that Jesus Christ is truly, substantially, and really present, Body, Blood, Soul, and Divinity, under the appearance of bread and wine in the Holy Eucharist. This is the truth that elevates the Mass above every other form of Christian worship and forms the bedrock of this entire book.

This presence is known as the **Real Presence**, and it occurs through the miracle of **transubstantiation**. When the priest says the Words of Consecration, the entire substance of the bread and wine is changed into the Body and Blood of Christ. The outward forms, the color, taste, and texture, remain, but the underlying reality is Christ Himself.

When you kneel at Mass, you are kneeling before God Himself. When you receive Holy Communion, you are receiving Jesus. Understanding this one profound truth is the difference between attending a ceremony and entering into an intimate, life-changing encounter with your Creator and Savior.

Why Understanding the Order of the Mass Helps You Participate More Deeply

For a beginner, the Catholic Mass can feel like a rapidly moving play performed in an unfamiliar language. You might wonder:

- *Why are we saying "Lord, have mercy" right now?*

- *Why does the priest wash his hands?*
- *What exactly is the "Mystery of Faith" and why are we shouting it?*

When the steps, gestures, and prayers are unknown, it's easy to feel lost and disconnected. However, the Mass is perfectly ordered, with a logic and flow that date back centuries. Every movement, every word, and every silence has a profound, scriptural, and historical meaning.

This guide will illuminate that order. By understanding *why* you stand for the Gospel, *why* you kneel during the Consecration, and *why* the priest's prayers are structured the way they are, you move from passively watching to actively praying. When you know the meaning, the Mass stops being a ritual and becomes a pilgrimage, a step-by-step journey with Christ Himself. This deep understanding allows you to participate with your mind and your heart, not just with your body.

What This Guide Covers

This pocket guide is structured into five accessible parts designed to take you from a curious observer to a deeply engaged participant:

- **Part I: Understanding the Holy Mass** lays the theological foundation, explaining what the Mass is and why it has this ancient structure.
- **Part II: The Order of the Catholic Mass** is the step-by-step guide, walking you through every movement of the Mass, from the Entrance Procession to the Final Dismissal, explaining the prayers and actions along the way.
- **Part III: Understanding the Prayers, Gestures, and Meaning** unpacks the rich symbolism, explaining why we stand, sit, and kneel, and revealing the meaning behind signs, bells, and silent moments.
- **Part IV: Practical Helps for a More Prayerful Mass** offers actionable advice on how to prepare for Mass, stay focused during it, and carry the grace of the Mass into your daily life.
- **Part V: Short Prayers and Devotions** provides simple, reverent prayers you can use before, during, and after receiving Holy

Communion.

How to Use This Book

This is not a book meant to be read once and shelved; it is a companion for your weekly journey.

1. **Read Part I and Part II first.** This will give you the complete landscape of the Mass.
2. **Bring it with you.** When you are at Mass, use Part II as a reference. As a particular section occurs, say, the Penitential Act, open to that chapter and read the brief explanation of its purpose to instantly deepen your focus.
3. **Study the symbols.** Use Part III during the week to ponder the gestures you see and perform.
4. **Practice the prayers.** Use the short prayers in Part V to transform your time before and after Communion from idle waiting into intentional, personal prayer.

Whether you are a newcomer to the faith, a lifelong Catholic who wants to renew their devotion, or simply curious about this ancient Christian liturgy, this book is for you. May this guide help you unlock the great treasure, encounter Christ fully, and discover why the Holy Mass is indeed the most important event of your life.

✠

1

What Is the Catholic Mass

When you first walk into a Catholic church, you are entering a space unlike any other. The ritual of the Holy Mass, the center of all Catholic life, is a majestic, multi-layered encounter. You will see structured prayers, hear ancient chants, and witness precise gestures, but to understand the Mass, you must look past the ritual and grasp the profound reality unfolding on the altar.

The Mass, formally known as the Eucharistic Celebration, is the highest form of prayer and the definitive act of worship in the Catholic Church. It is not simply a service or a community gathering; it is the moment when the eternal work of Jesus Christ is made present. To truly grasp its reality, we must see it through three inseparable, complementary lenses: **sacrifice, memorial, and sacred meal.**

The Mass as Sacrifice: The Unbloody Calvary

The word **"sacrifice"** is the most misunderstood aspect of the Mass. When we say the Mass is a sacrifice, we do not mean that the priest is re-crucifying Jesus or that Christ is being offered up as a victim again. Scripture is crystal clear: Christ died **"once for all"** (Hebrews 10:10). His sacrifice on the cross at Calvary was perfect, complete, and sufficient.

Instead, the Mass is the **unbloody re-presentation** of that single, eternal sacrifice. It makes the saving actions of Good Friday present *here and now*. Through the power of the Holy Spirit and the consecrated words of the priest, what happened on the cross two thousand years ago transcends time and space and becomes available to us on the altar. We are spiritually transported to the foot of the cross, where we join our prayers, our struggles, and our entire lives to Christ's perfect offering.

The priest, who acts **in persona Christi** (in the person of Christ), offers this divine sacrifice to God the Father for the forgiveness of sins, ours and those of the whole world. The altar is, therefore, not just a table but the spiritual altar of Calvary itself. This act of offering ensures that the infinite grace earned by Christ's death is poured out onto the world in every generation.

The Mass as Memorial: Connecting the Last Supper and Calvary

In common language, a "memorial" is merely an act of remembering a past event, like recalling a photograph or a birthday. However, in the biblical and liturgical sense (known as *anamnesis*), the word carries tremendous power: **it makes the past event effective and real in the present moment.**

The entire ritual of the Mass flows directly from the command Jesus gave his Apostles at the **Last Supper**: **"Do this in memory of me"** (Luke 22:19). This command was not simply a request to recall a nice meal. It was Christ's institution of the New Covenant, the moment He transformed the traditional Jewish Passover meal into the ultimate Christian celebration. At the Last Supper, Jesus anticipated and enacted His sacrificial death, giving His Body and Blood to His disciples *before* He physically died.

The Mass serves as the vital link connecting the Upper Room (the institution of the Eucharist) and the Hill of Calvary (the execution of the sacrifice). It is the perpetual fulfillment of Christ's presence, ensuring that His saving act is accessible to every person, in every age. When we celebrate the Mass, we are not just looking back; we are actively participating in the single, defining moment of human history.

The Mass as Sacred Meal: The Heavenly Banquet

Because the Mass is a sacrifice, it naturally leads to a shared, sacred meal. In the Old Testament, the consumption of a consecrated offering was the way the faithful entered into communion with God.

In the New Covenant, the Mass culminates in **Holy Communion**, where we, the faithful, receive the consecrated host and wine. Since the sacrifice offered is truly the Body and Blood of Christ (the Real Presence, achieved through transubstantiation), the Mass provides divine nourishment. This is the **spiritual food** necessary for eternal life, as Jesus taught: **"Truly, truly, I say to you, unless you eat**

the flesh of the Son of man and drink his blood, you have no life in you" (John 6:53).

This sacred meal is the deepest possible union we can achieve with Christ on earth. Receiving the Eucharist increases sanctifying grace, cleanses us from venial sins, and fortifies us against future temptation. Furthermore, the Mass is our greatest foretaste of the **Heavenly Banquet**, the perfect and eternal feast promised to the faithful in the Kingdom of God.

Scriptural Foundations

The roots of the Mass reach back to the earliest narratives of the Bible, showing that God always intended this form of worship:

- **Melchizedek (Genesis 14:18):** This mysterious figure, a priest and king who precedes the Mosaic Law, offered a sacrifice of **bread and wine**, a unique and direct prefigurement of the elements Christ would later choose for the Eucharist.
- **The Passover and Manna (Exodus):** The entire Jewish tradition of the Passover, where the blood of a lamb saved the firstborn, is

fulfilled by Christ, the **Lamb of God**, whose blood saves us all. The miraculous **manna** God provided in the desert (the "bread from heaven") is replaced by Christ, the true Bread of Life.

- **The Liturgy in Heaven (Revelation 4–5):** The Book of Revelation provides glimpses of the eternal liturgy of heaven, where the angels and saints offer unending praise around the throne of God and the **"Lamb standing, as though it had been slain."** The earthly Mass is our privileged participation in this eternal, heavenly worship.

In essence, the Catholic Mass gathers all of salvation history into one present moment, providing us with Christ's perfect sacrifice, His real presence, and His divine nourishment. It is truly the "source and summit" because all Christian activity flows from this union with Christ and is directed toward it.

✠

2

Why Catholics Attend Mass

As Chapter 1 revealed, the Mass is truly the re-presentation of Christ's sacrifice and the source of His real presence, now the question shifts from *what is it* to *why must I be there?*

For Catholics, attending Mass is not merely an option or a nice tradition; it is an essential duty of worship, a divine command, and a necessity for spiritual survival.

The Divine Command: Keeping the Lord's Day Holy

The obligation to gather for worship finds its deepest roots in the Old Testament: the **Third Commandment**. Given by God to Moses, it states: **"Remember the sabbath day, to keep it holy"** (Exodus 20:8).

For Christians, the Sabbath moved from the seventh day to the first day of the week, **The Lord's Day,**

Sunday, in celebration of Christ's Resurrection. The Resurrection of Jesus, which occurred on Sunday, transformed this day from one of simple rest into the primary day of Christian worship and rejoicing.

The Church, using the authority Christ gave her, formalizes this as the **Sunday Obligation**. It is the minimum requirement for a practicing Catholic to gather on Sunday (or the Saturday vigil Mass) to offer worship to God. By dedicating this day, we affirm that God is the rightful center of our lives, acknowledging Him as the source of all our blessings.

Christ's Command: "Do This in Memory of Me"

The second, even more profound reason for Mass attendance is simple obedience to Christ himself. When Jesus instituted the Eucharist at the Last Supper, His command was not passive: **"Do this in memory of me"** (Luke 22:19).

To attend Mass is to actively participate in the perpetuation of this New Covenant. Christ did not just ask us to think about Him; He gave us a specific, ritualized action, the Mass, by which we could continuously unite ourselves to His Passion and receive His grace. By gathering as a community, we fulfill His mandate and make His saving presence accessible to the world.

Why Sunday Mass Is Obligatory

The Church teaches that the Sunday Obligation is a **grave matter** because the Eucharist is the source of all spiritual life. To willfully miss Mass on a Sunday or Holy Day of Obligation, without a serious reason, is considered a mortal sin.

This rule is not about strict legalism; it's about the **gravity of the gift** being rejected. If God offers you the spiritual food necessary for eternal life, His very Body and Blood, to intentionally turn away from that gift is a profound act of spiritual negligence.

Valid reasons for missing Mass include serious illness, the need to care for a sick family member, or genuinely impossible circumstances like severe weather. If you are well enough to engage in normal weekend activities, you are well enough to prioritize the worship of God.

Spiritual Benefits: Nourishment and Grace

Beyond duty, Catholics attend Mass because of the

incomparable spiritual benefits that flow from the Eucharist:

- **Union with Christ (Holy Communion):** The primary benefit is the deepest possible physical and spiritual union with Jesus Christ. Receiving the Eucharist increases sanctifying grace and gives us the strength to resist temptation throughout the week.
- **Cleansing from Sin:** The Penitential Act cleanses us of venial (less serious) sins, preparing our hearts for a worthy reception of Communion.
- **Nourishment of the Word:** The Liturgy of the Word feeds our minds with Scripture and provides guidance through the Homily, illuminating how God's ancient truth applies to our modern struggles.
- **Community and Unity:** The Mass unites us not only with Christ but with the entire Church, past, present, and future. It is a visible sign of the unity of the Body of Christ.
- **Grace for Mission:** The Final Blessing sends us out empowered. We receive the "marching

orders" to live the faith we have celebrated, carrying the grace and peace of Christ into our daily lives and interactions.

In short, attending Mass is an act of love, obedience, and spiritual necessity. It is where God guarantees us the grace required to lead a holy life.

✠

3

How the Mass Is Structured

Having grasped the profound reality of *what* the Mass is, the next step in becoming an active participant is understanding its carefully planned architecture. The Catholic Mass is not a random sequence of events; it is a single, unified action of Christ, organized into a four-part journey that beautifully tells the story of salvation.

This structure, with minor variations, has been the framework for Christian worship since the earliest centuries.

The Four Major Parts of the Mass

The Order of the Mass is traditionally divided into four main segments, each fulfilling a necessary role in our worship and spiritual nourishment:

1. The Introductory Rites (Gathering and Preparation)

The purpose of this first section is to gather the people of God, foster a sense of community, and prepare our hearts and minds to celebrate the sacred mysteries worthily.

- **Key Action:** We move from our separate lives into a unified, sacred community.
- **Key Moment:** The **Penitential Act** is vital here, as it allows us to confess our venial sins and failures, clearing our hearts so we can listen to God's word and approach the altar with greater purity. The Rites conclude with the **Collect** (Opening Prayer), where the priest gathers all our silent intentions and offers them to God.

2. The Liturgy of the Word (Hearing God Speak)

This is the first major part of the Mass. Following the ancient tradition of the Jewish synagogue service, we sit down to receive instruction from the Sacred Scriptures. God is speaking to us through the human voice of the lector or deacon.

- **Key Action:** We listen attentively to God's

plan of salvation.

- **Key Moment:** The highest point is the **Gospel Reading**, which recounts the life and teachings of Jesus Christ. We stand out of reverence for Christ speaking directly to us. The **Homily** follows, applying the timeless Word of God to our specific lives today. We conclude this section by standing to profess our shared faith in the **Creed** and then praying for the needs of the world in the **Prayers of the Faithful**.

3. The Liturgy of the Eucharist (Sacrifice and Meal)

This is the true climax and central part of the Mass, fulfilling all the sacrifices of the Old Testament. Here, Christ's sacrifice on the cross is re-presented and we are nourished by His Body and Blood.

- **Key Action:** We participate in Christ's offering of Himself to the Father and then receive Him in Holy Communion.

- **Key Moment:** The **Eucharistic Prayer** is a single, unified prayer of thanksgiving that includes the **Words of Consecration**, which is the moment of *transubstantiation* (when the bread and wine truly become the Body and Blood of Christ). This is the reason we kneel, to adore the Real Presence of God. This entire section leads directly to the **Communion Rites**, including the communal praying of the **Lord's Prayer** and the reception of the Eucharist.

4. The Concluding Rites (Mission and Dismissal)

The final part of the Mass is the briefest, yet it is arguably the most action-oriented. We do not end the service by saying, "It is finished," but by being sent forth.

- **Key Action:** We receive a final blessing and are commissioned to take the grace we received out into the world.
- **Key Moment:** The **Dismissal** by the deacon or priest (e.g., "Go forth, the Mass is ended") is a charge to action. It confirms that the liturgy is not confined to the church walls; it is meant to be lived out daily.

Why the Mass Has This Order

The structure of the Mass is deliberate. It follows a logic that mirrors our relationship with God and even the ancient liturgical practice of the Jewish people:

1. **Purification (Introductory Rites):** We acknowledge our sinfulness and ask for God's mercy so we are fit to speak to Him.
2. **Instruction (Liturgy of the Word):** We allow God to speak to us through the Scriptures, preparing our minds for the great mystery.
3. **Worship and Communion (Liturgy of the Eucharist):** We respond to God's Word by offering Him the perfect sacrifice of His Son, and then He gives us Himself in return.
4. **Application (Concluding Rites):** We are sent out, strengthened by the Eucharist, to bring Christ's love and peace to the world.

Understanding this clear, four-step progression allows you to see the Mass not as a series of unrelated moments, but as a single, powerful act of encounter with the living Christ.

✠

4

Sacred Space and Sacred Items

When you step into a Catholic church, you enter a space that has been intentionally set apart, or **consecrated**, for the worship of God. Every item, every piece of furniture, and every vestment worn by the priest is steeped in symbolism and history, all pointing toward the central mystery of the Eucharist.

Understanding the key elements of this sacred space and the items used in the liturgy will greatly deepen your sense of reverence and participation.

The Sacred Space: The Sanctuary

The front section of the church, usually elevated by steps, is called the **Sanctuary**. This is the holy place where the sacred mysteries are celebrated. It is reserved for the clergy and ministers, signifying the special role they play in leading the worship. Within the Sanctuary, four elements are most crucial:

The Altar

The altar is the single most important piece of furniture in the church. It is not merely a table; it is the **altar of sacrifice**. It represents Christ himself, the Priest, the Altar, and the Victim.

- **Symbolism:** It is often made of stone, symbolizing Christ as the Cornerstone, and usually contains relics (physical remains) of saints, reminding us that the earthly Church is united with the heavenly Church.
- **Function:** It is the place where the sacrifice of the Mass is re-presented and where the bread and wine are consecrated.

The Ambo (or Pulpit)

The Ambo is the stand from which the Scriptures are proclaimed.

- **Symbolism:** It represents the table of the Word of God.
- **Function:** The Readings, the Psalm, and the Gospel are read from here, and the homily is often preached from here, signifying that the

Word of God is proclaimed with authority.

The Tabernacle

The Tabernacle (from the Latin for "tent" or "dwelling place") is the secure, ornamented repository where the consecrated Eucharist (the Body of Christ) is reserved outside of Mass.

- **Symbolism:** It is the "real presence" dwelling place, echoing the tent where the Ark of the Covenant was kept in the Old Testament.
- **Reverence:** A burning **Sanctuary Lamp** is always placed nearby. If the lamp is lit, it signifies that the consecrated host is present inside the Tabernacle. This is why Catholics **genuflect** (bend the right knee to the floor) toward the Tabernacle upon entering and leaving the church, it is an act of adoration toward Christ truly present.

The Presider's Chair

This is the chair reserved for the priest or bishop who is celebrating the Mass.

- **Symbolism:** It symbolizes the priest's role as the leader of the assembly and the one presiding over the worship in the person of Christ.

The Sacred Items: Vessels and Linens

The vessels used on the altar hold the precious Body and Blood of Christ and must be treated with the utmost care and reverence.

The Chalice

A large cup, usually made of gold or silver, used to hold the wine that will become the Blood of Christ.

The Paten

A small, shallow plate, also made of precious metal, used to hold the bread (hosts) that will become the Body of Christ.

The Ciborium

A covered, often ornate vessel used to hold the consecrated hosts for distribution during Holy Communion. The remaining hosts are stored in the Ciborium inside the Tabernacle.

Purificator and Corporal

These are special linens used on the altar.

- The **Corporal** (from *corpus*, meaning body) is

a large square cloth laid out under the chalice and paten.

- The **Purificator** is a small cloth used to wipe the lip of the chalice and clean the sacred vessels after Communion.

The Sacred Vestments: Layers of Meaning

The garments worn by the priest during Mass are called **vestments**. They are not simply robes; they are symbols that cover the ordinary personality of the man, allowing Christ the Priest to shine forth, and each piece has spiritual meaning rooted in ancient Roman or biblical garb.

The Alb

A long white garment worn by the priest (and often other ministers) that extends from the neck to the ankles.

- **Meaning:** Symbolizes the garment of innocence the priest received at his baptism.

The Stole

A long strip of cloth worn over the neck. The priest wears it crossed over his chest, while a deacon wears it diagonally over one shoulder.

- **Meaning:** Symbolizes the yoke of Christ's service and the authority of the priesthood.

The Chasuble

The large, outer garment worn over the Alb and Stole. It is usually the most colorful and ornate vestment.

- **Meaning:** Symbolizes the mantle of charity that covers all things. Its color changes according to the liturgical season (e.g., green for Ordinary Time, purple for Advent/Lent, white for Christmas/Easter).

Why Gestures and Symbols Matter

The physical items and the structured space remind us that we are engaged in a physical, tangible worship. God uses matter (water, oil, bread, wine, linen, stone) to communicate spiritual grace. When you understand what the altar represents or why the priest is wearing a specific color, the Mass transforms from a bewildering ritual into a rich, visual prayer experience. Every symbol is a signpost pointing toward Jesus Christ.

✝

5

Entrance Procession & Sign of the Cross

The moment the music begins and the priest and ministers process into the church, the Mass formally starts.

The Entrance Procession

The **Entrance Procession** is a powerful symbol. It is not just the clergy walking to their places; it represents Christ entering His Church, and it serves to gather the scattered faithful into one unified Body. The **Entrance Song** helps us transition from the world outside into the sacred event we are about to celebrate, fostering communal harmony and setting a joyful or penitential tone, depending on the season.

The procession culminates as the priest approaches the altar. He immediately shows reverence, often by kissing or deeply bowing to it. This act reminds us that the altar is not just a table, but a symbol of Christ Himself.

The Sign of the Cross

The priest then begins the Mass by leading everyone in the **Sign of the Cross** with the words: "In the name of the Father, and of the Son, and of the Holy Spirit. Amen."

This simple gesture is the most fundamental prayer of the Catholic faith. The words profess our belief in the **Holy Trinity**, and the physical motion traces the shape of the **Cross**, the definitive sign of Christ's love and our redemption. By starting the Mass this way, we dedicate the entire liturgy, and ourselves, to the Triune God, reminding us that we stand in the presence of the crucified and risen Christ.

✝

6

Greeting

Immediately following the Sign of the Cross, the priest extends a communal greeting to the assembly. This is not merely a polite "Hello"; it is a profound theological statement.

The Meaning of the Greeting

The priest typically says, **"The Lord be with you,"** and the assembly responds, **"And with your spirit."** This exchange is one of the oldest and most consistent parts of the Christian liturgy, repeated several times throughout the Mass.

The greeting serves as a reminder that Christ, who was invoked in the Sign of the Cross, is truly present in the midst of the gathered community and in the person of the priest, who acts in the spirit of his ordination. By responding, **"And with your spirit,"** the congregation prays that the grace, power, and office received by the priest through the Holy Spirit remains with him as he celebrates the Mass for them.

This exchange is a moment of faith, affirming that we are not alone in the church, but that the presence of the Holy Trinity and the grace of Christ's saving work are at the heart of our gathering. It formally concludes the opening rites of greeting and directs our focus toward the penitential preparation that follows.

✠

7

Penitential Act

Following the Greeting, the priest invites the assembly to participate in the **Penitential Act** (or *Penitential Rite*). This is a crucial moment of self-reflection and communal cleansing.

Purpose: Preparing Our Hearts

We are about to enter the most sacred part of the liturgy, the Liturgy of the Word and the Liturgy of the Eucharist. To participate worthily, we must first acknowledge our human failures and sinfulness. The Penitential Act serves to confess our venial (less serious) sins, allowing us to approach the altar with a contrite and purified heart. It is a necessary spiritual cleansing before we listen to God's Word and receive Christ Himself.

There are a few forms of the Penitential Act, but all include the collective prayer: **"I confess to almighty God..."** This act of confession is made to God, but also to "you, my brothers and sisters," reinforcing that our sins affect the whole Body of Christ.

Meaning of "Lord, Have Mercy"

The rite culminates in the repeated plea: **"Lord, have mercy (Kyrie eleison); Christ, have mercy (Christe eleison); Lord, have mercy (Kyrie eleison)."**

This is an ancient expression of prayer found in both the Bible and the earliest Christian liturgies. It is a humble cry from the heart, asking for the forgiveness necessary to proceed with the celebration. Through this collective act of repentance, the entire assembly receives a cleansing from God's infinite mercy, preparing us to move forward into the Liturgy of the Word.

✠

8

Gloria

Following the cleansing of the Penitential Act, the assembly is ready to offer a great hymn of praise to God, known as the **Gloria**.

A Heavenly Hymn

The opening lines of the Gloria are taken directly from the Gospel of Luke (2:14), echoing the song the angels sang to the shepherds on the night of Christ's birth: **"Glory to God in the highest, and on earth peace to people of good will."**

The rest of the prayer expands into a magnificent, ancient hymn of praise, acknowledging the Father, the Son (Jesus Christ), and the Holy Spirit. We joyfully worship God for His goodness and grace, moving beyond simply asking for mercy to celebrating His glory.

When We Say It (And When We Don't)

The Gloria is a characteristic part of Sunday Mass, but it is **omitted** during the penitential seasons of Advent and Lent. This exclusion helps mark these seasons as times of expectant waiting and quiet repentance. Similarly, it is not said on weekdays of Ordinary Time.

However, when the Gloria *is* sung or recited, its purpose is clear: it is a burst of communal adoration. It serves as a necessary transition, completing the Introductory Rites by lifting our hearts in unified praise, preparing us to sit and listen to God speak directly to us in the Liturgy of the Word.

✝

9

Collect (Opening Prayer)

The final piece of the Introductory Rites is the **Collect**, also known as the Opening Prayer. This prayer serves as the official transition from the preparation stage into the Liturgy of the Word.

The Priest Gathers Our Intentions

The priest introduces the Collect by saying, "Let us pray," often after a brief moment of silence. This silence is crucial; it is a moment for the assembly to mentally pause, recall why they are present, and privately offer their deepest personal intentions to God (for family, for strength, for those who are suffering, etc.).

The word "Collect" perfectly describes the priest's role: he is the one who **collects** all the individual, silent prayers of the faithful and synthesizes them into one cohesive petition. He offers this single prayer to God the Father, through Jesus Christ, in the

Holy Spirit.

Thematic Focus

The specific text of the Collect changes every day and is carefully chosen to reflect the theme of the day, the liturgical season, or the feast being celebrated. It often summarizes the entire spiritual focus of the Mass, giving the assembly a central thought to carry through the Liturgy of the Word. Once the priest concludes the Collect, the entire assembly responds with a definitive **"Amen,"** formally closing the Introductory Rites and preparing us to sit and listen to the Scriptures.

10

The First Reading

With the conclusion of the Introductory Rites, we now sit and formally enter the **Liturgy of the Word**, during which God speaks to His people. The priest, deacon, or a lay minister reads the first Scripture passage, typically taken from the **Old Testament**.

The Principle of Fulfillment

The choice of the First Reading is not arbitrary; it follows a powerful theological principle called **fulfillment**. On Sundays and major feast days, the First Reading is almost always selected because it anticipates, foreshadows, or helps explain the Gospel reading.

For instance, if the Gospel tells the story of Jesus curing a leper, the First Reading might be a passage from the Old Testament Law describing leprosy and God's instructions for purifying the unclean. The Old Testament serves as the foundation, and the New

Testament (the Gospel) reveals the fulfillment of God's plan in Christ.

Why We Sit

We sit during the readings to adopt a posture of **reception and meditation**. Just as students sit to learn from a teacher, we sit to listen and allow the ancient, inspired Word of God to penetrate our minds and hearts. We respond to the reading by saying, **"Thanks be to God,"** acknowledging the gift of Scripture we have just received.

✠

11

Responsorial Psalm

Immediately following the First Reading, the faithful participate in the **Responsorial Psalm**. This is not just another reading; it is a vital communal prayer and our direct response to the Word of God we just heard.

Praying Scripture

The Responsorial Psalm is almost always taken directly from the **Book of Psalms** in the Old Testament. The Psalms were the ancient prayer book and hymn book of Israel, and they are now the prayer book of the Church. By singing or reciting them, we unite our voices to the thousands of years of prayer that precede us.

The structure is simple: the cantor (or choir) sings the verses of the psalm, and the assembly replies with a repeated **Refrain** (or response). The refrain is carefully chosen to capture the main theme of the preceding First Reading. This structure ensures that the entire community actively meditates on the Scripture.

The Liturgical Function

The Psalm has a dual purpose: first, it provides a meditative bridge between the First Reading and the Second Reading, giving us time to digest what God has spoken. Second, it shifts the mode from listening (sitting) to praying and singing (sitting, or sometimes standing for the response). It is our heart's first verbal reply, affirming our acceptance of the truth and promise presented in the reading. It moves the Scripture from the page into our personal spiritual lives.

12

The Second Reading

After the meditative bridge of the Responsorial Psalm, we return to the Scriptures for the **Second Reading**.

The Apostolic Voice

For Sunday Masses and major feasts, the Second Reading is typically taken from the **New Testament Epistles** (letters), most often from the letters of Saint Paul, but sometimes from the writings of Peter, John, or James, or from the Book of Revelation.

Unlike the First Reading, which is chosen to connect thematically with the Gospel, the Second Reading usually follows a **semi-continuous pattern**. This means that over a period of several weeks, the readings proceed straight through a single book, offering a focused study on a particular Apostolic text. This allows the faithful to receive systematic teaching on Christian living and doctrine as taught by the Apostles.

The Purpose of the Epistles

The Epistles were written to the early Christian communities to instruct them on faith, morality, and how to live the Christian life. By hearing them read today, we receive the same spiritual guidance from the early Church.

As with the First Reading, we sit to listen, adopting the posture of disciples learning from the Apostles. We conclude this reading by once again saying, **"Thanks be to God,"** grateful for the Apostolic wisdom that guides our daily discipleship.

✝

13

Gospel Acclamation & Gospel

The Liturgy of the Word reaches its climax with the proclamation of the **Gospel**, which is preceded by a joyful sung preparation.

The Gospel Acclamation

We stand for the Gospel Acclamation, which is most often the **Alleluia** (meaning "Praise the Lord"). This is a brief, joyful cry of welcome. It serves as our energetic, verbal procession to meet Christ, who is about to speak to us directly in His own words. Just as a king is welcomed with fanfare, we welcome the King of Kings before His teachings are read. Like the Gloria, the Alleluia is omitted during Lent, replaced by a non-joyful verse of acclamation as a sign of penitence.

The Gospel Reading

The Gospel, read only by a priest or deacon, is the **high point** of the entire Liturgy of the Word. It comes directly from the four Evangelists: Matthew, Mark, Luke, or John.

We stand out of deep reverence, showing that we are ready to receive the words of Christ with immediate obedience. We also make the **triple sign of the cross** on our forehead, lips, and heart, praying that God's Word may be in our **mind** (that we may understand it), on our **lips** (that we may proclaim it), and in our **heart** (that we may live it). The Gospel is the most sacred text, and hearing it is the greatest instruction we receive at Mass.

✝

14

Homily

Immediately following the proclamation of the Gospel, the priest or deacon preaches the **Homily**. This is the only part of the Mass when the primary posture for the assembly is **sitting**, signifying that we are now students, ready to receive instruction.

Breaking Open the Word

The purpose of the Homily is simple: to **break open** the Word of God that has just been proclaimed. The Homily must be based on the Scripture readings or the liturgical feast of the day. It is the moment when the ancient, timeless truths of the Bible are applied directly to the contemporary life of the congregation.

The preacher takes the wisdom of the First Reading, the Responsorial Psalm, the Second Reading, and the Gospel, and explains how these truths should shape our thoughts, actions, and decisions in the week ahead. It moves the message from theory to practice.

Essential for the Liturgy

The Homily is not optional; it is a **required** part of the Liturgy of the Word on Sundays and Holy Days of Obligation. It is God's living voice continuing to guide His people through the ministry of the Church. By listening attentively, we ensure that the spiritual food of the readings is properly digested and integrated into our souls, preparing us to offer the great sacrifice that follows.

✝

15

The Creed (Profession of Faith)

After hearing the Word of God proclaimed and receiving instruction through the Homily, the assembly stands to recite the **Creed**, or Profession of Faith.

Why We Pray It Together

The Creed serves as the official, communal response to the Liturgy of the Word. Having listened to God's message, we now affirm our belief in the fundamental truths He has revealed. It is not just a recitation; it is a **public and collective declaration** of everything the Catholic Church holds to be true.

We typically recite the **Nicene Creed**, which was formulated at the Councils of Nicaea (325 AD) and Constantinople (381 AD) to precisely define the Church's teaching on the Holy Trinity and the divinity of Christ. On certain occasions, the shorter **Apostles' Creed** may be used.

The Defining Moment

During the recitation of the Creed, there is one key moment of reverence: we **bow** at the words **"and by the Holy Spirit was incarnate of the Virgin Mary, and became man."** This profound bow is a physical sign of deep respect and gratitude for the miracle of the Incarnation, the moment the eternal Son of God humbled Himself and became human for our salvation.

✠

16

Universal Prayer (Prayer of the Faithful)

The **Liturgy of the Word** concludes with the **Universal Prayer**, often called the Prayer of the Faithful. After God has spoken to us through the Scriptures and we have affirmed our faith in the Creed, we respond by speaking to God on behalf of the entire world.

Lifting Up the World

This prayer is universal because our concerns extend beyond ourselves and our own community. It is an act of intercession, where we exercise our priestly function as baptized Catholics to pray for the needs of others.

The intentions are always presented in a specific order:

1. **For the Church:** For the Pope, bishops,

priests, and all the faithful.

2. **For the World:** For civil authorities, those suffering war, and for peace and justice.
3. **For the Suffering:** For the poor, the sick, the marginalized, and the deceased.
4. **For the Local Community:** For the specific needs of the local parish and assembly.

Structure and Response

A lector or minister usually announces each intention, and the assembly replies with a communal response, such as **"Lord, hear our prayer."**

The Universal Prayer bridges the gap between the Word and the Eucharist. It reminds us that our faith is never private; it compels us to bring the needs of the whole world to the altar, where the greatest act of love, the Eucharist, is about to be offered for all.

By concluding the Liturgy of the Word, we transition from passively receiving God's instruction to actively confirming our assent to the faith, preparing us to move into the Liturgy of the Eucharist.

✝

17

Preparation of the Gifts (Offertory)

The **Liturgy of the Eucharist** begins immediately after the Prayer of the Faithful. This section, historically and popularly known as the **Offertory**, is where the altar is prepared and the gifts of bread and wine are brought forward.

The Symbolic Offering of Our Lives

This rite is far more than just setting up the table. The bread and wine brought to the altar represent the fruits of human labor, the wheat harvested and milled, the grapes pressed and fermented. But symbolically, they represent **us**. Just as the bread and wine are about to be transformed, we offer our work, our struggles, our joys, and our entire selves to God, asking Him to transform us as well.

During this time, the collection is usually taken up,

symbolizing the community's material support for the Church and the poor. Our monetary offering is joined to the primary offering of the bread and wine.

The Preparation of the Elements

As the gifts are brought forward, the priest performs several specific actions that are deeply symbolic:

1. **Preparation of the Bread:** The priest offers the paten, praying a blessing over the bread, acknowledging that it is the "fruit of the earth and work of human hands."
2. **Mixing Water and Wine:** The priest pours wine into the chalice, but then adds a tiny drop of water. This is an ancient and profound symbol. The **wine** symbolizes the divinity of Christ, and the **water** symbolizes our humanity. By mixing them, the priest recalls the union of Christ's divinity and humanity, and our own union with Christ in the Eucharist. The priest quietly prays that just as the water is mingled with the wine, "may we come to share in the divinity of Christ who humbled himself to share in our humanity."
3. **Washing of Hands (Lavabo):** The priest

washes his hands, saying quietly, *"Lord, wash away my iniquity, and cleanse me from my sin."* This ritual, called the *Lavabo*, is not for hygiene, but for spiritual purification. It is a powerful reminder that the minister must be inwardly clean to celebrate the great mysteries of the Mass.

Invitation to Prayer

The entire Preparation of the Gifts culminates with the priest asking the assembly to join in prayer: "Pray, brothers and sisters, that my sacrifice and yours may be acceptable to God, the almighty Father." The assembly replies, "May the Lord accept the sacrifice at your hands, for the praise and glory of his name, for our good, and the good of all his holy Church."

This exchange confirms that the upcoming sacrifice is not just the priest's act, but the corporate offering of the entire body of believers. We are now ready to enter the heart of the Mass: the Eucharistic Prayer.

✠

18

Eucharistic Prayer: The Heart of the Mass

The **Eucharistic Prayer** is the single most solemn and central moment of the entire Mass. Everything that came before, the Penitential Act, the readings, the Homily, has been preparing us for this moment. It is a long, unified prayer of thanksgiving and sanctification that is addressed entirely to God the Father.

The entire assembly stands during this prayer, adopting the ancient posture of honor and vigilance, acknowledging that we are offering our worship alongside the priest.

The Great Act of Thanksgiving

The Eucharistic Prayer is structured as one continuous action, moving from praise to petition, and finally, to the central act of the Mass.

1. The Preface Dialogue and Preface

The prayer begins with the **Preface Dialogue**, an ancient exchange between the priest and the assembly:

- **Priest:** "The Lord be with you."
- **People:** "And with your spirit."
- **Priest:** "Lift up your hearts." (We respond by raising our focus to heaven.)
- **People:** "We lift them up to the Lord."
- **Priest:** "Let us give thanks to the Lord our God."
- **People:** "It is right and just."

The priest then continues with the **Preface**, a beautiful prayer that gives thanks to the Father for all His works of creation and salvation, particularly through His Son.

2. The Sanctus (Holy, Holy, Holy)

The Preface concludes abruptly, leading to the **Sanctus**, or "Holy, Holy, Holy." This is the first climax of the Eucharistic Prayer, sung or recited by the entire assembly.

The words are taken from the prophecies of Isaiah (6:3) and the Gospel of Matthew (21:9). By singing the Sanctus, we unite our voices with the angels, archangels, and all the saints in heaven, who are eternally praising God. It is the moment when the earthly Mass joins the timeless, unending liturgy of heaven.

3. The Epiclesis (Calling Down the Spirit)

Following the Sanctus, the priest extends his hands over the bread and wine and asks God the Father to send down the Holy Spirit to consecrate the gifts. This moment, called the **Epiclesis** (Greek for "invocation"), is crucial. We acknowledge that the transformation requires the direct intervention of the Holy Spirit, who makes the bread and wine holy.

4. The Institution Narrative and Consecration

This is the heart of the Mass. The priest recounts the actions and words of Jesus at the Last Supper: **the Institution Narrative.** The priest speaks the very words of Christ, "This is my Body... This is the chalice of my Blood...", acting *in persona Christi* (in the person of Christ).

At these words, the miracle of **transubstantiation**

occurs: the entire substance of the bread and wine is changed into the Body and Blood of Christ. The outward appearance remains, but the underlying reality is God Himself. The bells ring, and the priest elevates the consecrated host and chalice for the silent adoration of the faithful, who kneel in profound reverence.

✠

19

The Lord's Prayer

Following the conclusion of the Eucharistic Prayer (the great sacrifice), the liturgy shifts its focus entirely to the meal aspect of the Eucharist. We are preparing to receive Holy Communion, and this preparation begins by reciting the prayer Jesus himself taught us: **The Lord's Prayer (or the Our Father).**

The Family Prayer

The Lord's Prayer is unique. While the Eucharistic Prayer is reserved for the priest, the Our Father is the first prayer in the Liturgy of the Eucharist spoken entirely by the entire assembly. We pray it together, standing and often holding hands, signifying that we are one family, children of the same Father, united in preparation for the sacred banquet.

By calling God "Our Father," we acknowledge our adoptive relationship with Him, made possible through Christ, and our common brotherhood with everyone in the Church. It is the perfect summary of all Christian prayer, encompassing praise, petition, and a request for divine grace.

Asking for Daily Bread

The most important petition in this context is, **"Give us this day our daily bread."** While this plea certainly refers to our physical sustenance, liturgically and spiritually, it is a fervent prayer for the **Eucharist** itself. It is a request for Christ, the *Bread of Life*, to sustain us through the day and into eternity. This petition confirms that we recognize the Eucharist as the necessary spiritual food for our journey.

Praying for Forgiveness and Peace

The subsequent petition, **"And forgive us our trespasses as we forgive those who trespass against us,"** serves as a final, vital act of spiritual cleansing before receiving Communion. Jesus taught us that we cannot receive God's forgiveness if we are unwilling to extend forgiveness to others. This prayer challenges us to reconcile any grudges or bitterness, ensuring our hearts are open to the peace of Christ. If we know we are in a state of mortal sin, this prayer reminds us that sacramental Confession is necessary before receiving the Eucharist.

The Embolism

The priest immediately follows the Lord's Prayer with a special petition called the **Embolism** (from the Greek word meaning "insertion"). He takes the final phrase of the Our Father, "Deliver us from every evil", and elaborates on it, praying: *"Deliver us, Lord, we pray, from every evil, graciously grant peace in our days..."*

The Embolism makes explicit the Church's prayer for liberation from sin, fear, and spiritual peril, and asks for the gift of peace while we await the coming of Christ. It seals the intentions of the Our Father and prepares the way for the Sign of Peace that immediately follows, concluding the first step of the Communion Rites.

✠

20

Sign of Peace

Following the communal recitation of the Lord's Prayer and the priest's Embolism, which asks for deliverance from evil and the gift of peace, the liturgy reaches a crucial moment of communal preparation: the **Sign of Peace**.

The Theological Necessity of Peace

The Sign of Peace is not merely a custom or a social break; it is a profound theological necessity derived directly from Christ's teaching in the Gospel of Matthew: **"If you are offering your gift at the altar, and there remember that your brother has something against you, leave your gift there before the altar and go; first be reconciled to your brother, and then come and offer your gift"** (Matthew 5:23–24).

Before we can receive the ultimate gift, Jesus Christ in the Eucharist, we must actively seek reconciliation and demonstrate Christian charity toward our neighbors. We are about to be united with Christ, the head of the Body, and therefore, we must show solidarity and peace with all the members of His Body, the Church. The peace we share is not merely human peace, but the divine peace of Christ himself, which surpasses all earthly understanding.

The Priest's Prayer for Unity

The rite begins with the priest praying a beautiful prayer addressed to Christ: *"Lord Jesus Christ, who said to your Apostles: Peace I leave you, my peace I give you; look not on our sins, but on the faith of your Church, and graciously grant her peace and unity in accordance with your will. Who live and reign for ever and ever. Amen."*

This prayer reveals the true purpose of the Sign of Peace: it is a prayer for the **unity and peace of the entire Church**, not just the local congregation. It is an acknowledgment that true peace comes only from Christ and that only His forgiveness can overcome division.

The Action and Gesture

After the priest invites the assembly to exchange the

Sign of Peace ("The peace of the Lord be with you always... Let us offer each other the sign of peace"), the people turn to exchange a brief gesture. In many cultures, this is a handshake; in others, it might be a nod or a slight bow.

The gesture should be brief, simple, and reverent. It is not the time for long conversations or extended socializing. The focus remains on the sacred action unfolding on the altar. The gesture is a formal way of saying: "I am reconciled with you, and I wish you the peace of Christ as we both prepare to receive Him."

The Sign of Peace brings the assembly into the right disposition: spiritually cleansed by the Penitential Act, strengthened by the Word, and now reconciled with one another, we are truly ready to participate in the climax of the Liturgy of the Eucharist.

✝

21

Lamb of God

The brief, repetitive prayer known as the **Lamb of God** (*Agnus Dei*) is one of the most powerful and meaningful moments just before Holy Communion. It is an act of deep humility and a final communal preparation to receive the consecrated host.

Biblical and Historical Origin

The title **"Lamb of God"** has profound biblical roots:

1. **The Passover Lamb (Old Testament):** In the Book of Exodus, the blood of the spotless lamb, spread on the doorposts, saved the Israelites from the Angel of Death. This event, the original Passover, foreshadowed Christ's sacrifice.
2. **John the Baptist (New Testament):** When John the Baptist saw Jesus coming toward him, he declared, **"Behold, the Lamb of God, who takes away the sin of the world!"**

(John 1:29). This proclamation identified Jesus as the fulfillment of the Passover sacrifice, the spotless victim whose blood would truly save humanity from sin and death.

By repeating the prayer, **"Lamb of God, you take away the sins of the world, have mercy on us,"** we recall Christ's sacrificial identity, confess our need for His mercy, and acknowledge His unique power to cleanse the world.

The Fraction Rite (Breaking of the Bread)

While the assembly sings or recites the *Agnus Dei*, the priest performs the **Fraction Rite**, the physical breaking of the consecrated Host. This action is rich with symbolism:

- **Echoing the Last Supper:** Breaking the bread recalls the actions of Jesus at the Last Supper and the practice of the early Church, which referred to the Mass simply as "the breaking of the bread" (Acts 2:42).
- **Symbol of Sacrifice and Unity:** The breaking of the one Host signifies Christ's Body being broken for our sake on the Cross. Yet, by sharing the pieces among many, it also

symbolizes the unity of the faithful, who are made one Body by sharing in the one Bread.

The Commingling

After the breaking, the priest places a small piece of the consecrated Host into the chalice. This is called the **Commingling** or **Mixture** (*Immixtio*).

This action symbolizes the reunion of Christ's Body (the Host) and Blood (the wine in the Chalice) after the separation that occurred at His death. It represents the **resurrection** of Christ, reminding us that we receive the *living* and *glorified* Christ, Body, Blood, Soul, and Divinity, in the Eucharist.

The three-fold repetition of the "Lamb of God," coinciding with these sacred actions, ensures our hearts are perfectly disposed to receive the Lord who comes as a sacrificial victim, a source of peace, and resurrected life. The final plea, **"grant us peace,"** is a request for the true peace of God that Holy Communion alone can provide.

✝

22

Holy Communion

After the preparations of the Lord's Prayer, the Sign of Peace, and the "Lamb of God," the moment arrives for the faithful to approach the altar and receive **Holy Communion**. This is the climax of the entire liturgy, the sacred meal where we receive the consecrated Host, which is truly the Body, Blood, Soul, and Divinity of Jesus Christ.

Approaching the Real Presence

Because we believe in the **Real Presence** (the teaching that the consecrated bread and wine are no longer bread and wine, but Christ Himself), receiving Communion demands utmost reverence.

- **State of Grace:** The first and most critical prerequisite is that a Catholic must be in a state of **grace**. This means having no knowledge of any unconfessed mortal (serious) sin. If a mortal sin has been committed since the last confession, a person must reconcile through the Sacrament of Penance (Confession) before receiving the Eucharist.

- **Fasting:** Canonical law requires Catholics to fast from all food and drink (except water and medicine) for at least one hour before receiving Holy Communion. This small sacrifice highlights the importance of the spiritual nourishment we are about to receive.

The Moment of Reception

As you approach the minister, you will either kneel or stand (depending on local custom). Before receiving, you should make a clear gesture of reverence, usually a profound bow of the head.

The minister holds up the Host and says, **"The Body of Christ."** You should respond clearly and firmly, **"Amen."** This "Amen" is a public declaration of faith: *"I believe that what you hold is truly the Body of Christ, and I assent to receiving Him."*

The Host can be received either on the tongue or in the hand. If receiving in the hand, the custom is to place one hand over the other, creating a throne for the Lord, and immediately consume the Host in front of the minister before turning to leave.

Prayers of Thanksgiving

Once back in your seat, the time immediately following Communion is one of the most precious moments of the Mass. This is the **time for Thanksgiving**.

Instead of immediately jumping into the final prayers, the faithful are encouraged to spend this time in silent prayer, recognizing the extraordinary gift they have received. Christ is literally dwelling within you. This time is best spent in adoration, gratitude, and petition, asking Christ to use the grace you have received to strengthen you for the week ahead. It is an opportunity for deep, personal union with God.

✝

23

Final Blessing & Dismissal

The Mass does not conclude after Holy Communion. Following the silent time of thanksgiving, the liturgy enters the **Concluding Rites**, which serve to wrap up the sacred celebration and, crucially, to commission the faithful to live out the graces they have received.

1. Post-Communion Prayer (The Second Collect)

The priest first leads the assembly in the **Post-Communion Prayer**. Similar to the Opening Prayer, the priest invites the faithful to pray silently before he offers a concluding prayer. This prayer is focused on the gift just received, the Holy Eucharist.

- **Purpose:** It is a collective prayer of gratitude for the spiritual nourishment of Christ's Body and Blood. It typically asks God to help the assembly apply the grace of this sacrament to their daily lives, ensuring that the spiritual food they received bears tangible fruit.

- **Function:** This prayer formally closes the Liturgy of the Eucharist and prepares the assembly for dismissal.

2. Final Blessing

Before the final word is spoken, the priest raises his hands and invokes God's blessing upon the people.

The blessing is often given in the most ancient form: "May Almighty God bless you, the Father, and the Son, and the Holy Spirit. Amen." This reminds us that we are sent forth fortified by the grace of the **Holy Trinity**, the same divine Persons we invoked at the beginning of Mass during the Sign of the Cross. This blessing is the source of strength we take with us as we re-enter the secular world.

3. The Dismissal: Go Forth, the Mass is Ended

The very last exchange of the Mass is also one of its most important: the **Dismissal**. The deacon or priest typically says one of four formulas, all carrying the same meaning: **"Go forth, the Mass is ended,"** or **"Go and announce the Gospel of the Lord."**

The word "Mass" itself comes from the Latin *Ite, missa est*, which translates roughly to **"Go, it is the sending (dismissal)."**

This is not a permission to leave; it is a **mission**. The Church does not want us to stay enclosed within the walls of the building. The grace, peace, and spiritual strength we have received are meant to be shared. The Dismissal sends us out into the world, our homes, workplaces, and communities, to be living witnesses of Christ's presence and love. We are commissioned to carry the Mass into our everyday lives.

The assembly's response, **"Thanks be to God,"** expresses gratitude for the gift of the Mass and signals their acceptance of this divine mission. The priest and ministers then reverence the altar one last time and process out, bringing the celebration to a close.

✝

24

Why Catholics Stand, Sit, and Kneel

If you are new to the Mass, the constant shifting of postures, standing, sitting, kneeling, can be confusing. However, these movements are not arbitrary; they are deeply symbolic actions that convey reverence, readiness, and humility. The collective movement of the assembly into these three postures is a visible expression of our shared faith and participation in the liturgy.

Standing: The Posture of Resurrection and Readiness

Standing is the primary posture for prayer and is the most common posture used in the ancient Church.

- **Resurrection:** For Christians, standing is the posture of the **Resurrection**. We stand because we believe Christ has conquered death and we, too, are destined for eternal life. It signifies hope and triumph. It is a visible rejection of the ancient practice of kneeling in sorrow or mourning; we stand upright as children of God, redeemed by Christ.

- **Readiness and Respect:** Standing also indicates a posture of **respect and readiness** to act. We stand whenever the priest or deacon reads the Gospel, because we are preparing to hear the words of Christ himself with immediate obedience. We stand for the opening and closing prayers, the Creed, and the Final Blessing, moments that require us to be active participants in the mission of the Church.
- **When We Stand:** We stand for the Introductory Rites (Entrance, Penitential Act, Gloria, Collect), the Gospel reading, the Profession of Faith (Creed), the Universal Prayer, and the Concluding Rites (Final Blessing and Dismissal).

Sitting: The Posture of Learning and Meditation

Sitting is the traditional posture of the student listening to the teacher.

- **Meditation and Reception:** When we sit at Mass, we are taking on the role of **disciples**, ready to receive instruction. It is the posture for listening and meditating on the Word of God. By sitting, we settle down, focus our minds, and allow the message of the Scriptures and the Homily to penetrate our hearts.
- **Comfort for Long Texts:** Sitting also provides the necessary physical comfort to focus on the content of the longer readings and the Homily without distraction.
- **When We Sit:** We sit for the First Reading, the Responsorial Psalm (though the response may be sung standing), the Second Reading, and the Homily. We also sit during the Preparation of the Gifts (Offertory) as the altar is prepared, and during the silent period of Thanksgiving following Holy Communion.

Kneeling: The Posture of Adoration and Supplication

Kneeling is the most profound posture of **reverence, worship, and humility** in the Catholic tradition.

- **Adoration:** We kneel before God to acknowledge His supreme authority and our utter dependence on Him. This is the posture reserved for moments of direct contact with the divine presence.
- **The Consecration:** The most important time for kneeling is during the **Eucharistic Prayer**, specifically from the *Sanctus* (Holy, Holy, Holy) until the Doxology ("Through him, and with him..."). We kneel during the Consecration to adore Christ present in the consecrated Host and Chalice. It is an act of recognizing the great miracle of transubstantiation unfolding before us.
- **Supplication:** Kneeling is also the posture of **supplication**, meaning earnest prayer or petition. When we kneel, we are physically humbled, expressing the deepest poverty of our spirit before the Lord, asking for His

mercy and grace.

- **When We Kneel:** Traditionally, we kneel for the entire Eucharistic Prayer, and often for the Penitential Act. We also genuflect (a brief kneeling on one knee) toward the Tabernacle upon entering or leaving the pew, recognizing Christ reserved in the Eucharist.

Postures as Prayer

The sequence of these postures tells a story: we **stand** with the confidence of the Resurrection, **sit** to receive instruction, **kneel** to adore the King, and finally, **stand** to receive His blessing and be sent forth on our mission. By unifying these physical actions, the assembly prays not just with words, but with the entire body.

The physical act of changing posture reminds us that the Mass demands our full engagement, mind, soul, and body, in the sacred liturgy.

✝

25

Signs, Symbols, and Gestures

The Catholic Mass is a profoundly sensory experience. It involves speaking, hearing, standing, sitting, kneeling, and seeing, all of which draw our entire being into the act of worship. The actions and sacred items used, beyond the central drama of the Eucharist, are known as **sacramentals** and **gestures**. They are the rich, silent language of the liturgy, designed to communicate deep theological truths that words alone cannot express.

The Sign of the Cross: Our Identity and Redemption

The **Sign of the Cross** is the most frequent and defining gesture in the Mass. It is done not only at the very beginning and end of the liturgy but also at the Gospel reading and during the Concluding Rites.

This simple act is a dual profession of faith:

1. **Trinitarian Faith:** The words, "In the name of the Father, and of the Son, and of the Holy Spirit," affirm our foundational belief in the Holy Trinity.
2. **Redemption:** The physical motion, tracing the shape of the cross over our body, reminds us that we are redeemed by Christ's sacrifice on Calvary. It is a spiritual mark, identifying us as baptized Christians and invoking God's protection over the entire assembly and the action about to take place.

It is a visible, physical act of prayer that consecrates the entire liturgy, marking every part of the Mass with the sign of salvation.

Reverence and Adoration: Bowing and Genuflecting

The ways we show physical reverence are not interchangeable; they reflect different levels of adoration and respect:

Genuflection

Genuflection (bending the right knee to the floor) is

reserved for Christ truly present in the Eucharist.

- **Required Use:** Every time a Catholic enters or leaves a pew where the **Tabernacle** (containing the reserved Eucharist) is present, they genuflect toward it. This is a personal act of adoration towards the Real Presence of Christ. During Mass, if the route to the altar does not pass the Tabernacle, one may genuflect before taking their place in the Sanctuary.

Bowing (Profound and Simple)

A bow is a lesser gesture of reverence, used for holy people and sacred items, not for God himself.

- **Profound Bow (Bow of the Body):** This deep bow from the waist is used during moments of significant humility or high respect.
    - *Examples:* Bowing during the Penitential Act as we confess our sins, or during the Creed at the words "was incarnate of the Virgin Mary." The priest also makes a profound bow to the altar when genuflection is not required.

- **Simple Bow (Bow of the Head):** This is a simple bending of the head used when the three Divine Persons are named together ("Glory to the Father, and to the Son, and to the Holy Spirit") and when bowing before receiving Holy Communion (before the minister says, "The Body of Christ").

Sacred Elements: Engaging the Senses

The use of elements like incense, bells, and holy water engages our senses and elevates the worship from the mundane to the sacred.

Incense

Incense (a fragrant smoke created by burning resins) is used in solemn Masses and processions.

- **Symbolism:**
  - **Prayer Rising:** The rising smoke symbolizes the prayers of the faithful ascending to God (Psalm 141:2, Revelation 8:4).
  - **Honor:** It is used to honor sacred persons (the priest) and sacred objects (the altar, the Gospel book, the

consecrated Eucharist).

    - **Cleansing:** It suggests the purification of the space and the faithful.

- **Use:** The altar and the gifts are often incensed during the Offertory, setting them apart for the great sacrifice.

Bells

The ringing of the **Altar Bells** has two primary purposes during the Eucharistic Prayer:

1. **Attention:** To draw the attention of the faithful to the most sacred moments of the Mass, the **Consecration.**
2. **Adoration:** Bells are rung as the priest elevates the consecrated Host and Chalice, providing a joyful, audible sign of the miracle of transubstantiation and inviting the faithful to kneel and adore the Real Presence of Christ.

Holy Water

Holy Water is water that has been blessed by a priest, invoking God's blessing upon it.

- **Symbolism:** It reminds us of our **Baptism,**

through which we became members of Christ's Body.

- **Use:** Catholics dip their fingers in the fonts placed at the entrances of the church and make the Sign of the Cross upon entering. This gesture is a renewal of our baptismal vows, cleansing us spiritually and preparing us to participate in the Eucharist. On occasion, the priest will bless the entire assembly with Holy Water during the Introductory Rites, replacing the Penitential Act.

Movement and Mission: Processions

The various **processions** in the Mass (the Entrance, the Gospel, the Offertory, and the Recessional) symbolize the Church's journey through history. We are not a static people; we are the pilgrim people of God, moving toward our eternal home. Every procession reminds us that the Church is always active and on mission. The final **Recessional** specifically reminds us that our worship is finished, and we are now sent out, commissioned, to carry Christ into the world.

These signs, symbols, and gestures transform the

Mass into a physical, living prayer, ensuring that every part of us, mind, soul, and body, is actively engaged in the worship of God.

✝

26

Silent Moments in the Mass

In a world filled with constant noise and chatter, the Mass might seem like a rapid flow of action and spoken prayer. However, woven into the liturgy are crucial, intentional periods of **silence**. These moments are not pauses for transition or waiting; they are integral parts of the worship experience, designed to allow the faithful to respond internally to the grace being offered.

Silence in the liturgy is a time when the external noise of the world is shut out, allowing the quiet voice of God to be heard and the depths of the human heart to speak.

Where Silence Occurs and Why

The General Instruction of the Roman Missal (GIRM) explicitly mandates periods of silence at specific points in the Mass, each with its own purpose:

1. At the Beginning (After "Let Us Pray")

Before the **Collect (Opening Prayer)** and the **Post-Communion Prayer**, the priest invites the assembly, "Let us pray," followed by a moment of silence.

- **Purpose:** This silence allows the faithful to gather their individual intentions, making a personal commitment to the prayers of the Mass. It is a time for private petition, which the priest then unites and offers to God in the communal prayer.

2. After the Readings and Homily

Immediately following each of the three readings and the Homily, a brief silence is essential.

- **Purpose:** This is a time for **meditation and internalization**. It allows the assembly to "digest" the Word of God they have just heard. Instead of immediately moving on, the silence ensures the Scriptures sink from the ears to the heart, giving the Holy Spirit space to illuminate how the Word applies to one's life.

3. After Holy Communion (Thanksgiving)

This is arguably the most important period of silence in the entire Mass. It occurs after the faithful have received the Body and Blood of Christ.

- **Purpose:** This is the **time for Thanksgiving**. With Christ dwelling physically within them, the faithful are encouraged to spend this time in profound, personal adoration and intimate dialogue with the Lord. It is a moment of deep, spiritual union, a time to express gratitude for the gift received and to ask for the grace to live as Christ's disciples.

The Necessity of Internal Prayer

These pockets of silence confirm that the Mass is not a spectator sport. It demands active participation that is both external (speaking and kneeling) and **internal** (listening and meditating). Without the silence, the liturgy risks becoming a shallow ritual where the words are heard but not truly received.

By embracing the silence, we make room for grace, transforming the Mass from a public ceremony into a truly personal encounter with the living God. It is in the quiet that we transition from communal hearing to individual conversion.

✠

27

Why the Mass Sometimes Feels Repetitive

For many, especially those who attend weekly, the greatest hurdle to full participation in the Mass is the feeling of **repetition**. The priest says the same prayers, the assembly gives the same responses, and the gestures, standing, sitting, kneeling, always follow the same order. If God is infinite, shouldn't our worship be constantly new and surprising?

Understanding the Catholic perspective on ritual is essential, for what may feel like "repetition" is, in fact, **ritual**, and ritual is one of the most powerful tools God uses to form us spiritually.

Ritual vs. Routine

It is important to distinguish between a **routine** and a **ritual**.

- A **routine** is a mechanical, often mindless

action performed simply to get a task done (e.g., brushing your teeth).

- A **ritual** is a carefully constructed sequence of actions, words, and symbols that is performed to connect the mundane world with a sacred, timeless reality.

The Mass is not a routine; it is the sacred ritual Christ commanded us to perform ("Do this in memory of me"). The very constancy of the ritual is what makes it effective.

The Purpose of a Fixed Ritual

Why does the Church insist on using the same words and same order every week?

1. Making the Mystery Present (The Memorial)

As discussed in Chapter 1, the Mass is the re-presentation of Calvary. It is a sacrifice that transcends time. If the Mass changed radically every week, we might focus on the human creativity of the celebrant rather than the divine action of Christ. The fixed nature of the prayers ensures that, regardless of the year, the day, or the priest, the central action, Christ's sacrifice, is faithfully and validly brought into the present. The ritual is the vehicle that carries us back to the Last Supper and the Cross.

2. Speaking a Universal Language

The constancy of the ritual ensures that if a Catholic from America attends Mass in Rome, Kenya, or Australia, they are instantly at home. They hear the same prayers (translated into the local language), see the same actions (the breaking of the bread, the elevation of the Host), and participate in the same responses. Repetition creates a **universal, unifying language of prayer** that binds the entire global Church across cultural and geographical divides.

3. Creating Sacred Time and Space

Ritualistic repetition separates the time of worship from ordinary time. When we stand for the Gospel or kneel for the Consecration, we are performing actions unique to this sacred space and time. This fixed order acts like a spiritual anchor, pulling us out of our busy, chaotic lives and into the stable, eternal reality of God's presence. The predictability is comforting; it allows our minds to relax their focus on the external world and turn inward.

How Repetition Forms Us Spiritually

The true genius of the Mass's repetitive structure lies

in its power to form Christian virtue over time. The repetition is not meant to be boring; it is meant to be **formative.**

1. Shifts Focus from Novelty to Presence

In a culture obsessed with novelty and entertainment, repetition forces us to confront a different spiritual truth: the extraordinary power of the **ordinary**. Since the words never change, we cannot rely on being entertained or surprised by new content. Instead, we are forced to ask: *What new meaning can I find in these familiar words today?*

This shifts the focus from the human action (what the priest or choir is doing) to the Divine Presence (what Christ is doing). The depth of our experience depends entirely on the depth of our intention, not the uniqueness of the liturgy.

2. Builds Spiritual Habit and Virtue

Spiritual growth is based on habit, not sudden bursts of effort. Just as physical discipline builds muscle memory, ritual repetition builds *spiritual memory*. By bowing at the Incarnation in the Creed, kneeling at the Consecration, and confessing our sins in the Penitential Act *every week*, these gestures of humility, adoration, and contrition become ingrained habits of the soul.

3. Encourages Deeper Meditation

Repetition allows for deeper meditation. Because you already know the words of the *Gloria* or the *Sanctus*, your mind is free to move beyond simple comprehension and begin to chew on the meaning. You are no longer reading the prayer; you are *praying* the prayer.

- This week, "Lord, have mercy" might be a dry recitation.
- Next week, after a personal failure, "Lord, have mercy" becomes an urgent, heartfelt plea.
- The week after, following a blessing, "Lord, have mercy" is a grateful acknowledgement of unmerited grace.

The prayer is the same, but the person praying it is different, and thus, the depth of the experience changes dramatically.

Conclusion: Embracing the Familiar

Rather than seeing the repetition of the Mass as a

flaw, we should view it as a profound gift. It is the steady, unmoving foundation upon which our spiritual lives are built. It is the promise that every week, in every Catholic church, Christ stands ready to repeat His gift of self to us, requiring only that we bring a renewed, open heart to the familiar prayers. The richness of the Mass is found not in change, but in the timelessness of its unchanging reality.

✠

28

How to Prepare Before Mass

The Catholic Mass is a divine encounter that requires more than just showing up. To fully enter into the sacred mysteries, the preparation we make *before* the Mass begins is nearly as important as our active participation *during* it. Just as an athlete prepares their body and mind before a competition, or a student prepares for an exam, we must prepare our hearts for our weekly encounter with Christ.

This chapter outlines three essential steps you can take in the minutes and hours leading up to the liturgy to transform your experience from a routine obligation into a profound act of worship.

1. Arrive Early and Embrace the Silence

The most practical step you can take is to **arrive at church early**. Aim for at least ten to fifteen minutes before the Entrance Procession begins.

- **Transition Time:** This early arrival provides crucial **transition time**. When you rush in just as the music starts, your mind is still caught up in the traffic, the search for a parking space, or the conversation you just had. Arriving early allows you to shed the distractions of the world and allow the sacred atmosphere of the church to settle your soul.
- **Respect for Others:** Arriving late disrupts the quiet prayer of those already present and draws attention to yourself rather than the altar. Early arrival is an act of charity toward your fellow worshippers.
- **Personal Prayer:** Use those quiet minutes before Mass to pray. Sit, kneel, or simply observe the Sanctuary Lamp and make a mental or spoken act of adoration toward Christ reserved in the Tabernacle. This time allows you to establish a connection with God *before* the communal prayers begin.

2. Set an Intention for the Mass

Before the Introductory Rites begin, it is incredibly

helpful to mentally or quietly offer a specific **intention** for the Mass you are about to attend.

- **Focus Your Attention:** Setting an intention helps you combat distraction, providing an anchor for your thoughts throughout the liturgy. When your mind begins to wander (and it will!), you can gently bring it back by recalling the specific person or need you are praying for.
- **Joining the Sacrifice:** The Mass is a sacrifice offered for the needs of the living and the dead. By offering a specific intention, for a sick family member, for a personal struggle, for peace in the world, or for the souls in Purgatory, you are actively joining your personal offering to Christ's perfect sacrifice on the altar.
- **Making it Personal:** The intention makes the Mass personal. Instead of feeling like you are simply reciting communal prayers, you know that the merit of this particular Mass is being applied to the specific needs of someone you love, or to the specific grace you need to

conquer a vice.

3. Prepare Your Heart: Spiritual Cleansing

Spiritual preparation is the most profound step. This involves consciously acknowledging your spiritual state and seeking God’s mercy.

- **The Moral Obligation:** As noted in Chapter 22, if you are aware of any **mortal (serious) sin**, you must reconcile through the Sacrament of Penance (Confession) before receiving Holy Communion.
- **Act of Contrition:** Even if you are not conscious of mortal sin, every day we commit numerous venial sins and minor failings. Take a moment before Mass to make an **Act of Contrition** (a heartfelt expression of sorrow for sin). You might pray: "Lord, I am sorry for all the ways I have failed you and my neighbor this week. Cleanse my heart and prepare me to receive your Word and your Body."
- **Reading the Scriptures:** For those who want deeper preparation, read the Mass readings for the day beforehand. This prevents the Word of God from hitting your ears for the

first time in the church. By reading them once at home, you allow your mind to be primed, so that when the lector proclaims the text, you are already listening for the Holy Spirit's specific message for you.

By practicing these steps, you transform the hour before Mass from a frantic rush into a peaceful time of spiritual gathering, ensuring that when the priest says, "In the name of the Father, and of the Son, and of the Holy Spirit," your heart is ready to respond.

✝

29

How to Stay Focused During Mass

Distraction is perhaps the most common struggle for anyone attending Mass, whether they are newcomers or lifelong Catholics. The sacred reality of the liturgy is profound, but our human minds are prone to wandering, thinking about our grocery list, worrying about work, or simply being distracted by a crying baby two pews over.

Full, conscious, and active participation requires diligence. The key is not to eliminate distraction entirely (which is impossible) but to train your mind to **gently redirect** its attention back to the altar and the divine action unfolding there.

1. Handling Internal and External Distractions

When a distraction arises, treat it like a mosquito:

acknowledge its presence, but do not swat at it, as swatting only draws more attention to it.

- **External Distractions:** If you hear an unavoidable noise or see something distracting, do not let your mind dwell on it. Immediately shift your gaze back to the priest, the altar, or the crucifix. Remember that the presence of Christ in the Eucharist transcends any environmental noise. Use the distraction as a spiritual cue: *"My mind wandered. I need to refocus on my intention."*
- **Internal Distractions:** If your mind drifts to a worry or a to-do list, offer that worry to God as a brief, silent prayer. Say, "Lord, I offer this worry about X to you," and then consciously bring your attention back to the prayer the priest is currently saying. By offering the distraction to God, you turn a moment of distraction into an act of prayer.

2. Praying with Your Body

Your physical body can be a powerful tool for centering your mind. Use the postures and gestures of the Mass (Chapter 24 and 25) to anchor your concentration.

- **Conscious Posture:** When you **stand**, stand tall, fully upright, as a vigilant, resurrected soul. When you **sit**, adopt the posture of a disciple, ready to learn. When you **kneel**, feel the weight of humility and adoration in your joints.
- **Intentional Gestures:** Never perform the Sign of the Cross, the genuflection, or the triple cross before the Gospel mechanically. Focus entirely on the act. When you touch your forehead, lips, and heart for the Gospel, concentrate on the prayer: *"May God's Word be in my mind, on my lips, and in my heart."* Let the physical act force the mental focus.

3. Simple Mental Prayers for Key Moments

One of the best ways to stay focused is to use short, repeatable mental prayers that align with the specific moment in the liturgy. These mini-prayers fill the mental void that distractions often occupy.

- **During the Readings:** Since you are sitting and listening, say a quiet prayer of petition: *"Lord, help me hear what you want me to* *know today."*

- **During the Penitential Act:** As you strike your breast, pray: *"Jesus, Son of David, have mercy on me, a sinner."*
- **During the Consecration:** As the priest elevates the Host, focus intently and whisper the powerful prayer of faith: *"My Lord and my God!"* (The exact words of St. Thomas the Apostle).
- **Before Holy Communion (Waiting in Line):** Pray the words of the Roman centurion: *"Lord, I am not worthy that you should enter under my roof, but only say the word and my soul shall be healed."* (This prayer is said immediately before the priest, but it serves well while waiting).
- **During Communion:** The time of receiving and the walk back to your pew is for deep adoration. Pray simply: *"Jesus, I love you. Increase my faith."*

4. Uniting Your Heart to the Priest's Prayers

Recognize that the priest is praying *on your behalf.* Your goal is to make his words your own.

- **Conscious Responses:** Do not rush the responses. When the priest says, "The Lord be with you," really mean it when you reply, **"And with your spirit."** When he concludes a major prayer, ensure your **"Amen"** is a full-hearted assent: "Yes, I believe it. So be it."
- **Embrace the Silence:** Use the moments of silence (after the Homily, after the readings) for their intended purpose: internalization. Do not use them to catch up on planning or worrying. Use them to reflect: *What was the one word or phrase from the reading that struck me?*

By utilizing these tools, conscious redirection, physical focus, mental mini-prayers, and active assent, you train your heart to resist distraction and enter fully into the timeless reality of the Mass.

✝

30

What to Do After Mass

The final words of the Mass, **"Go forth, the Mass is ended,"** are a definitive command. Yet, for many, the moments immediately following the Mass can feel rushed and often distracting. We must remember that the Concluding Rites do not signal the end of a religious obligation, but the beginning of a divine mission.

The way we leave and the way we behave immediately after Mass are crucial to ensuring the grace we received in Holy Communion is not instantly lost to the clamor of the world.

1. Post-Mass Thanksgiving (Stay and Pray)

Just as silence is encouraged immediately after receiving Communion, it is beneficial to remain in the pew for a few minutes after the Final Blessing and Recessional.

- **Reverence for Christ:** Christ is still truly

present in your soul, having just been received in the Eucharist. Leaving immediately, or using the final blessing as a cue to rush for the door, can feel like disrespecting a great guest.

- **The "Fifth Act" of the Mass:** Many spiritual writers call the time spent in prayer after Communion the "Fifth Act" of the Mass. Use this quiet moment to reinforce your relationship with Christ. Express profound gratitude, reaffirm your faith in His Real Presence, and offer Him your full self. A simple, personal conversation with the Lord is perfect here: *"Thank you, Jesus, for giving yourself to me. Stay with me today."*
- **Silence for Others:** Maintaining silence as you leave your pew and exit the nave shows reverence for the presence of Christ in the Tabernacle and respect for the people around you who may still be praying.

2. Offering the Graces of the Mass

The graces received at Mass are meant to be used. As you exit the church, make a conscious effort to dedicate the spiritual strength you have acquired to a specific purpose.

- **Apply the Message:** Recall the key takeaway from the Homily or one phrase from the readings. Ask Christ: *"How can I live this word today?"* Dedicate the next few hours to practicing that one virtue or truth (e.g., patience, charity, forgiveness).
- **Praying for Mission:** Offer the graces of the Mass for a specific person or cause outside the church walls. For example, *"I offer this Communion, Lord, for the conversion of my friend,"* or *"I offer this grace for the strength I need to be a better spouse today."* This ensures that the benefits of the Mass flow outward into the world.

3. Living the Dismissal

The command, "Go forth," or *Ite, missa est*, must be taken literally. The Church sends you out, transformed by the Eucharist, to make Christ present in the ordinary activities of your daily life.

- **The Church's Mission:** You are now a carrier of Christ. Your words, actions, and reactions, in traffic, in your job, or with your family, should reflect the peace and love you received at the altar.

- **Continuous Presence:** The Mass is not an escape from the world; it is the spiritual fuel that empowers you to face the world. The goal is to make your entire life a seamless continuation of the worship you experienced in church. The Mass never truly "ends" until you are back in God's presence in eternity.

By slowing down, consciously praying, and intentionally embracing your mission, you ensure that the spiritual power of the Mass transforms your entire week.

✝

31

Prayers Before Mass

As discussed in Chapter 28, preparation is key to active participation. Having a ready, short prayer can help you silence the distractions of the world and set your heart on the altar as you wait for the Mass to begin.

Below are simple prayer options, from the traditional to the more spontaneous, that you can use in the quiet minutes before the Entrance Procession:

1. Simple Invocation (Focus on Purity)

This prayer asks God to cleanse your heart and mind, ensuring you can hear the Word and receive the Eucharist worthily.

> "Lord Jesus Christ, I believe that I am about to participate in the great sacrifice of your Body and Blood. Cleanse my heart from all venial sin and worldly distraction. May my presence here today

honor your sacrifice and prepare me to receive your grace. Send your Holy Spirit to open my ears and my heart. Amen."

2. The Traditional Prayer of St. Thomas Aquinas

This is a deep prayer for worthy reception, often prayed by priests but fitting for all the faithful.

> "Almighty and ever-living God, I approach the Sacrament of your only-begotten Son, our Lord Jesus Christ. I come as one infirm to the physician of life, as one unclean to the fountain of mercy, as one blind to the light of eternal brightness. I ask your infinite generosity to heal my sickness, wash away my stain, enlighten my blindness, and enrich my poverty. Grant me to receive the Bread of Life with such reverence and contrition that it may be a safeguard to my soul, and a help to eternal life. Amen."

3. Spontaneous Intention Setting

If a formal prayer feels too complicated, use this time

to speak simply to God about your intention for the Mass.

> "Heavenly Father, I offer this entire Mass today for [Name a specific person or cause]. I ask that the graces of Christ's sacrifice be applied to [the need]. Help me to be patient, focused, and grateful throughout this hour, and to carry the peace of Christ out to the world when the Mass is ended. Amen."

By using one of these simple prayers, you establish a spiritual perimeter around your heart, making the transition from the secular world to the sacred mysteries smooth and focused.

✝

32

Prayers Before Communion

The few minutes leading up to Holy Communion, from the Sign of Peace through the Lamb of God and the priest's preparation, are the final opportunity for immediate spiritual readiness. This brief period should be used to intensify faith, humility, and desire for Christ.

When the priest says the crucial prayer, "Behold the Lamb of God... Blessed are those called to the supper of the Lamb," and the assembly responds, we are speaking two of the most important lines of the entire Mass. Your response should be prayed slowly and sincerely.

1. The Prayer of the Centurion

This is the response immediately following the priest's invitation. It is taken directly from the Gospel (Matthew 8:8), spoken by the Roman centurion to Jesus, demonstrating profound faith and humility:

> "Lord, I am not worthy that you should enter under my roof, but only say the word and my soul shall be healed."

This prayer acknowledges three truths: our **unworthiness** due to sin, Christ's **divine power** to heal us spiritually, and our complete **faith** in His word.

2. A Simple Act of Faith

As you proceed down the aisle to receive the Host, your heart should be burning with faith, moving beyond mere words to pure adoration. Use this short declaration to center your mind:

> "Jesus, I believe you are truly present in this Host. I adore you. Come into my heart and purify me."

3. Prayer for Purity and Union

A traditional, short prayer that focuses on asking for grace and union with Christ:

> "From your most precious wounds, O Lord, shelter me. Do not permit me to be separated from you. In the hour of my death, call me and bid me come to you,

that with your saints I may praise you forever. Amen."

The use of these brief prayers ensures that when the minister says, **"The Body of Christ,"** your response of **"Amen"** is not merely a formality, but a sincere, final declaration of faith and desire for spiritual union. This quiet preparation transforms your reception of the Eucharist from a quick physical movement into a profound act of divine love.

✝

33

Prayers After Communion

The moments immediately following the reception of Holy Communion are the most sacred of the entire Mass. Christ is physically present within you, making this the optimal time for intimate, personal prayer, a time known as **Post-Communion Thanksgiving**.

Do not rush this moment. Use the quiet time before the Post-Communion Prayer to focus entirely on the Guest you have just received. Below are a few simple ways to structure your prayer:

1. Act of Adoration and Gratitude

Focus on the majesty of Christ and the humility of His presence within you. This prayer is simple and heartfelt.

> "Soul of Christ, sanctify me. Body of Christ, save me. Blood of Christ, inebriate me. Water from the side of Christ, wash me. Passion of Christ, strengthen me.

Good Jesus, hear me. Within your wounds hide me. Permit me not to be separated from you. From the wicked foe defend me. At the hour of my death call me, and bid me come to you, that with your saints I may praise you forever and ever. Amen."

2. A Simple Dialogue (Spontaneous)

If formal prayer is difficult, simply speak to Jesus who is dwelling in your heart.

> "Lord Jesus, thank you for coming to me. I believe, I adore, and I love you. Please remain with me today and strengthen me so that I may be patient, humble, and charitable to everyone I meet. Use my hands and my words to bring your peace into the world."

3. Prayer for Grace to Live the Mission

This prayer asks that the grace received transforms your life and empowers you to fulfill the mission of the Mass.

> "Divine Physician, I have received the

medicine of immortality. Let this Communion not be for my judgment, but for the remission of my sins and the strengthening of my soul. Make me worthy, O Christ, to be a living sanctuary where your Holy Spirit may reside, and through me, reach others who need your love. Amen."

This period of thanksgiving is a powerful way to seal the graces of the Mass, ensuring that your spiritual union with Christ endures throughout your week.

✝

34

Prayer After Mass

Once the Mass is formally concluded with the Dismissal, and the priest has processed out, the final piece of the spiritual journey is the dedication of the grace received. Having spent a few moments in silent thanksgiving (Chapter 33), a brief closing prayer helps seal the experience and consciously accepts the mission to live the Mass in the world.

This final prayer transforms the act of leaving the church into an act of commissioning.

A Closing Prayer for Mission

The following prayer is simple, focusing on the intention to carry the peace and presence of Christ into the day's activities:

> "Lord Jesus, I have been nourished by your Word and strengthened by your Body. As I leave this sacred place, I ask you to go with me. Let your grace be a

constant light in my mind and a burning charity in my heart.

Where I encounter impatience, let me bring your peace.

Where I face discouragement, let me bring your hope.

I dedicate this Mass and all its graces to [Name a specific need or person you will encounter today]. May the memory of your presence keep me from sin and fill me with courage to be a true witness to the Gospel.

May the Father, the Son, and the Holy Spirit guide and protect me. Amen."

The Final Sign of the Cross

As you leave your pew, dip your fingers into the Holy Water font (Chapter 25) and make a slow, reverent Sign of the Cross. This final gesture is a spiritual action that reminds you of three things:

1. **Baptismal Identity:** You are renewing your commitment to Christ, begun at your Baptism.
2. **Protection:** You are invoking the Trinity's

protection as you leave the sanctuary and enter the challenges of the world.

3. **Mission:** You are marking yourself as a disciple sent forth from the Mass to live a life of grace.

By concluding your time in the church with this final dedication and the Sign of the Cross, you ensure that the spiritual power of the Mass is not left behind but is actively carried out into your daily mission.

✠

Conclusion

Living the Mass Daily

You have now journeyed through the structure, meaning, prayers, and practical help necessary to fully understand and participate in the Holy Mass. We began by establishing that the Mass is the single most important action in the Catholic life, and we end with a reaffirmation of the truth expressed in the Concluding Rites: **The Mass does not end; it sends us out.**

The phrase, *Ite, missa est*, "Go, you are sent", is the definitive summary of our spiritual calling. The goal of every Eucharist is not to make us better worshippers in a church building, but to make us better Christians in the world.

The Liturgy After the Liturgy

The Mass provides the spiritual fuel, but our daily life is the mission field. To **live the Mass daily** means consciously carrying the graces received in Holy

Communion into every moment of your week. This continuous spiritual life is often called "The Liturgy After the Liturgy."

It requires asking yourself three simple questions when you walk out of the church doors:

1. **How did I receive the Word?** Did the Homily or the readings strike a particular truth? That truth is your specific assignment for the week. If the Word challenged you to forgive, your mission is reconciliation. If it called you to charity, your mission is to seek out a hidden need.
2. **How did I receive Christ?** The love you experienced when you received the Body of Christ must be reflected in your dealings with others. The same peace that settled your heart during the silence of thanksgiving is the peace you are commissioned to bring into tense family dynamics, difficult meetings, and frustrating situations.
3. **How can I make my life a gift?** Every Mass is a perfect sacrifice of praise. Your life, too, is meant to be a daily offering. When you endure

a hardship with patience, serve a neighbor without complaint, or offer a moment of spontaneous gratitude, you are transforming your ordinary life into a spiritual sacrifice, uniting it with the one perfect sacrifice of Christ on the altar.

A Call to Consistency and Growth

Understanding the Mass is a lifelong process. The prayers and rituals will remain the same, but you will always be growing and changing. What felt confusing today will feel comforting next month. What felt repetitive last year will feel profoundly meaningful this year.

Don't be discouraged by distraction or dryness. Spiritual growth is not about feeling intense emotions; it is about **consistency**. It is about showing up, making the effort, and trusting that Christ keeps His promise to be present and to transform you, even when you feel least worthy.

By embracing the Mass as the wellspring of your faith, the ultimate source of truth, grace, and life, you ensure that the sacrifice of the altar truly becomes the driving force of your life. Go forth, fortified by the

Holy Eucharist, and announce the Gospel by the way you live.

A Note of Thanks

Thank you for allowing this guide to be a companion on your spiritual journey. It is my sincere hope that these pages have helped pull back the veil on the beauty of the Liturgy, allowing you to encounter Christ more deeply every time you step into a church.

Share Your Thoughts

If this guide has helped you or a loved one understand the Mass better, please consider leaving a review on Amazon. Your feedback not only helps other readers discover this resource but also supports the mission of spreading a deeper love for the Holy Eucharist.

May God bless you on your journey toward Him.

9 789357 797399

Printed at Repro India Ltd.